CREATIVE COLORING
FOR GROWN-UPS

SCANDINAVIAN
FOLK PATTERNS

METRO BOOKS
New York

METRO BOOKS
New York

An Imprint of Sterling Publishing
1166 Avenue of the Americas
New York, NY 10036

Designed by Ana Bjezancevic
Cover Illustration by Cindy Wilde

Illustrations by Angela Porter, Angelea Van Dam, Cindy Wilde, Felicity French, Hannah
Davies, James Newman Gray, Jo Taylor, Julie Ingham, Rosalind Monks, Sally Moret,
Sam Loman and Shutterstock.

ISBN 978-1-4351-6098-9

For information about custom editions, special sales, and premium and corporate purchases,
please contact Sterling Special Sales at 800-805-5489 or specialsales@sterlingpublishing.com.

Manufactured in China

4 6 8 10 9 7 5

www.sterlingpublishing.com

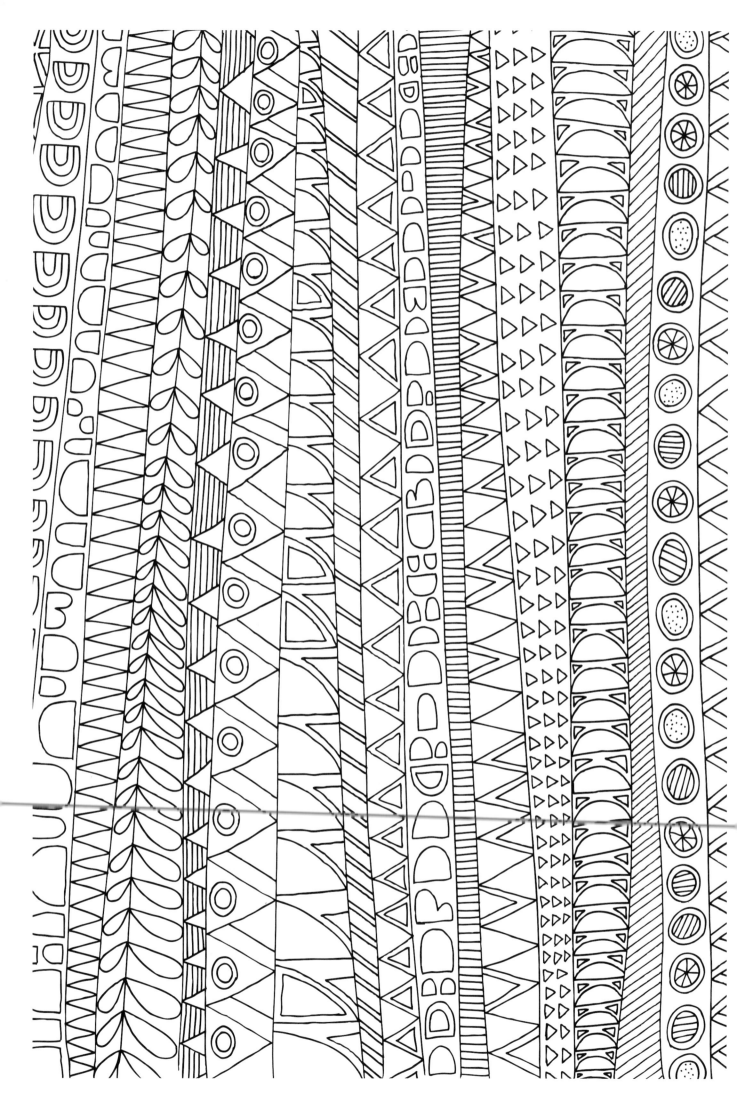

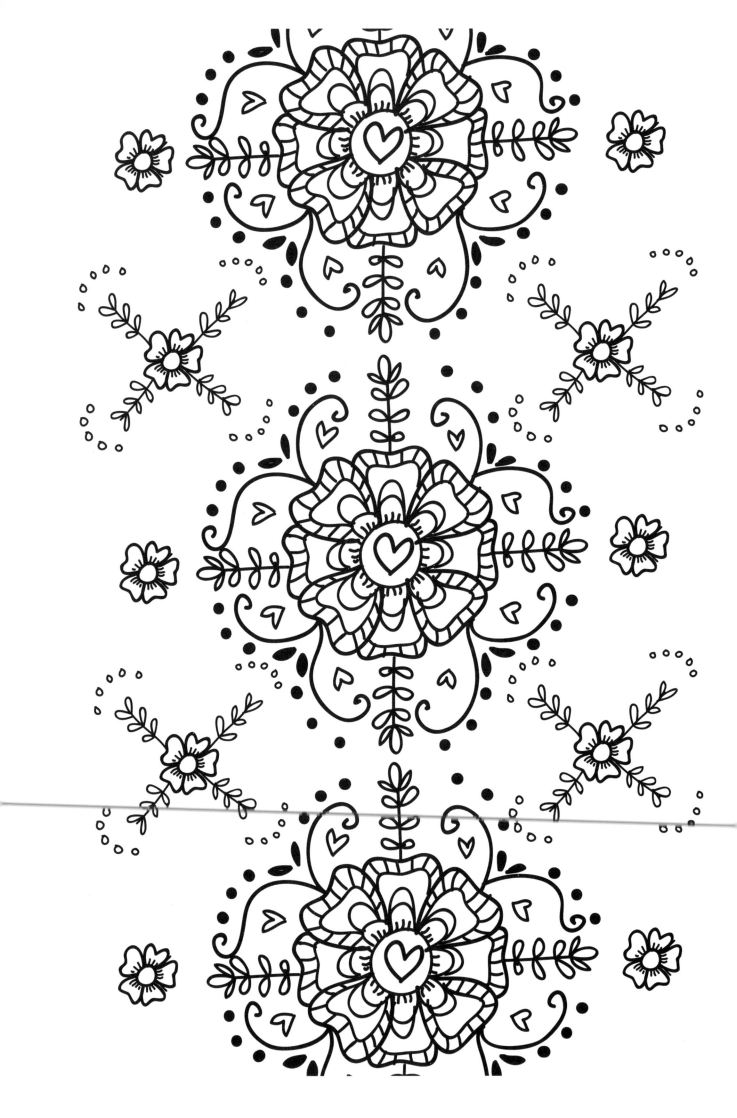

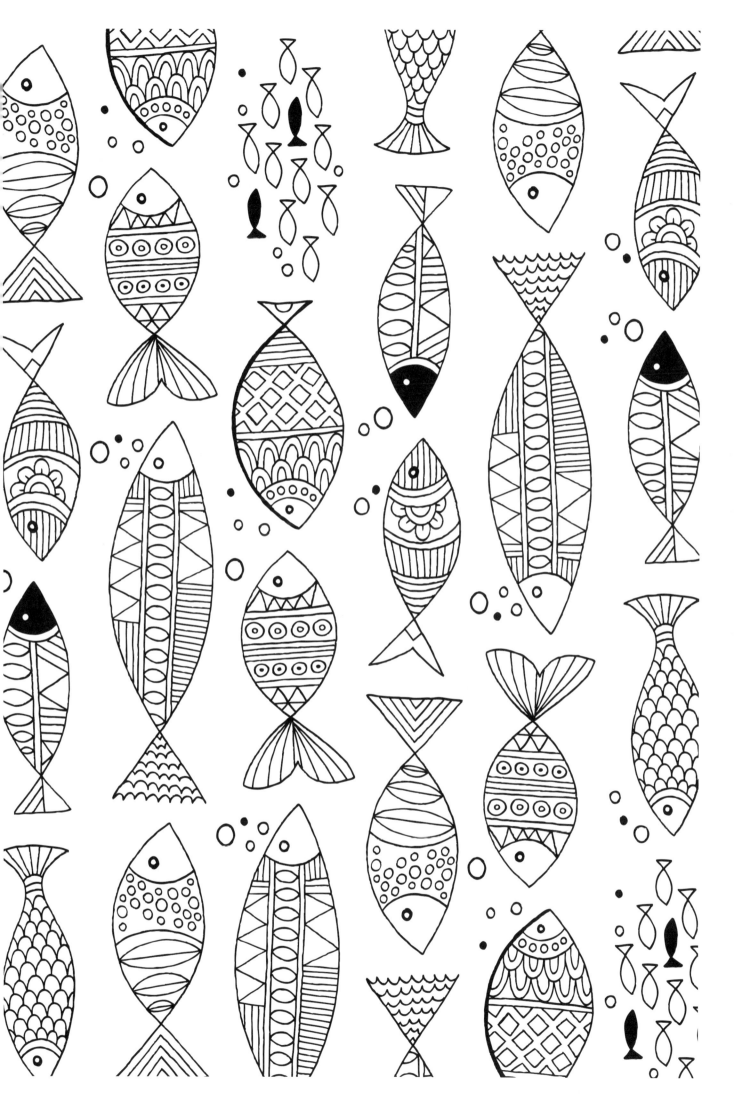

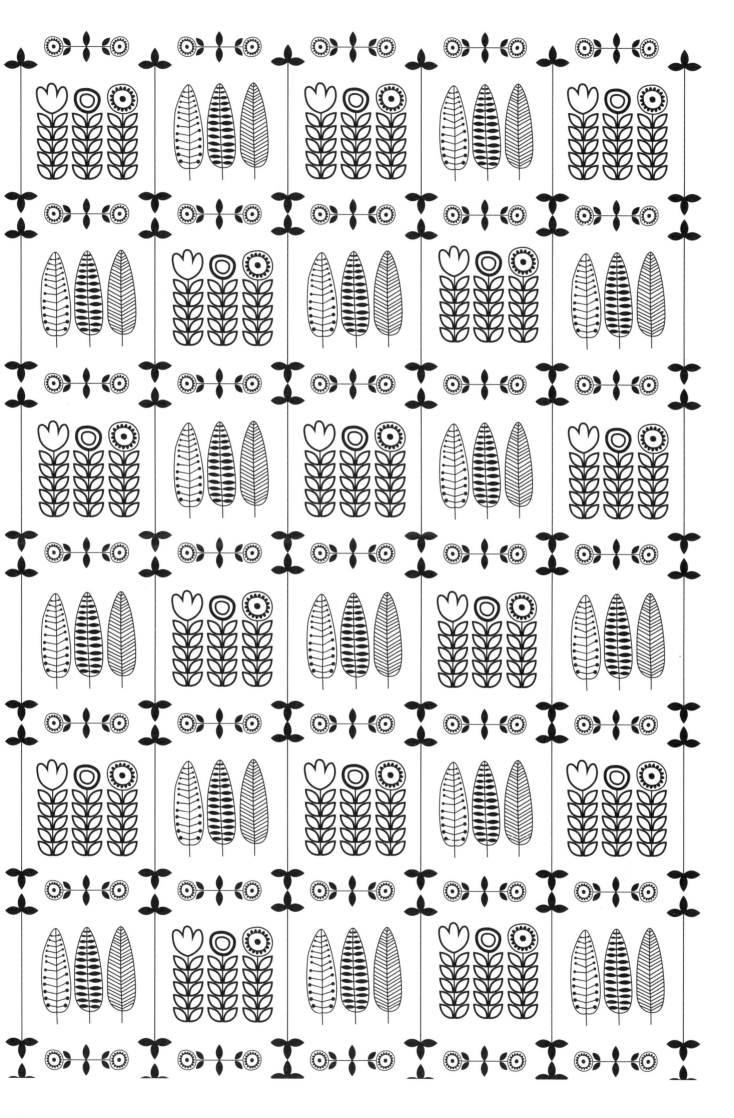